MY WEE GRANNY'S

BANNOCKS AND BAKES

BY

ANGELA HOSSACK

Also by Angela Hossack

My Wee Granny's Old Scottish Recipes

Dedicated to my Wee Granny

Annie Clarke

1890 – 1971

Contents

Introduction

My wee granny lived and cooked through two world wars. Ingredients weren't always plentiful but her delicious recipes – learned at her own mother's knee – stand testament to her skill and her ability to reach everyone's heart through their stomachs.

These recipes are the ones she used and the ones she passed down to her daughter – my big granny – and to my mother and then to me. I hope to pass them onto my own granddaughter and, although she is only three years old, she has already stood on a chair at the table and made her first cup cakes (or fairy cakes as my wee granny would call them).

The recipes in this book are plain and simple, but delicious.

Unfortunately – unlike my wee granny, my big granny and my mother – I don't have the cold hands necessary for a brilliant pastry chef, but I get by with my warm ones.

My first book – My Wee Granny's Old Scottish Recipes – has recipes across the whole eating experience, whilst this book concentrates on the baked goods all five generations of my family loved and love.

Bannocks

Bannocks can be either leavened (with baking powder or baking soda added) or unleavened (similar to a flatbread). They can be savoury or sweet.

They are a simple, traditional bread originating in Scotland and can be made outside on a fire on a bannock stane (stone), indoors on a griddle. Or in the oven.

It can be griddled dry, baked or fried using flour, barley or oatmeal.

Barley Bannocks

Serves 4-6

<u>What you will need</u>:

250mls of milk

Pinch of salt

1 tablespoon of butter

Half a cup of barley meal

Tablespoon of flour

<u>What you will need to do</u>:

Bring the milk to the boil with the butter and the pinch of salt. Stir the barley meal in quickly and stir continuously until it makes a dough.

Flour a board and turn out the dough. Roll out thinly and cut into 6 rounds.

Ideally you need a hot girdle, but a large non-stick frying pan will do. Bake on the hot girdle or the hot frying pan, turning once.

Eat hot.

Pitcaithly Bannocks

Serves 6

What you will need:

115g of butter

A pinch of salt

100g of caster sugar

1 cup of flour

A tablespoon of rice flour

A tablespoon of mixed peel

A tablespoon of flaked almonds

What you will need to do:

Cream the butter and sugar together and mix in the flour and the pinch of salt. Add the mixed peel and the flaked almonds.

Roll out into a cake about 13mm thick. Pinch the edges and place on a greased baking tin.

Bake in a moderate oven for about 30 minutes and cool on a wire tray.

Ardentinny Drop Bannocks

Serves 6

<u>What you will need</u>:

1 egg

500mls of milk

Half a teaspoon of baking soda

A pinch of salt

3 tablespoons of oatmeal

<u>What you will need to do</u>:

Beat the egg in a large bowl and stir in the milk. Mix in the baking soda and the salt, then mix in the oatmeal and stir until it forms a medium consistency batter.

Lightly grease a pre-heated griddle or heavy frying pan and drop a spoonful of mixture onto the heated pan. Repeat.

You will see the mixture rise and bubble as it cooks. Turn when golden (after about a minute) and brown gently on the other side.

Oat Bannocks (version 1)

Serves 4

<u>What you will need</u>:

2 tablespoons of butter

1 cup of course oats

A quarter of a cup of whole fat milk

Half a teaspoon of salt

<u>What you will need to do</u>:

Melt the butter in a pan and add the milk

Warm through and add the salt and the oats and mix thoroughly

With floured hands, turn the mixture out onto a floured board and split into 4 equal portions. Flatten and cook on a lightly greased griddle or heavy frying pan for a minute on each side.

Oat Bannocks (version 2)

Serves 6

<u>What you will need</u>:

1 cup rolled oats

1 cup oat flour

A quarter of a teaspoon salt

6 tablespoons of chilled unsalted butter

Half a cup of milk

1 egg yolk

<u>What you will need to do</u>:

Mix together the oats, oat flour and sugar and break in and mix through the butter.

Add the milk and mix thoroughly until a dough is formed, then on a floured board, roll out the mixture and put on a greased baking tray. Gently mark the top into squares

Brush the egg yolk over the top and bake for 20 minutes in a moderate oven (180 degrees C)

Oat Bannocks (version 3)

Serves 4

<u>What you will need</u>:

1 and a half cups of cold, cooked porridge oats

1 and a half cups of self-raising flour

A quarter of a teaspoon salt

6 tablespoons of chilled unsalted butter

A quarter of a cup of milk

A teaspoon of baking soda

<u>What you will need to do</u>:

Mix the flour, salt and baking soda with the cooked porridge and mix thoroughly.

Add the milk and form into a sticky dough

Turn out onto a floured board, roll out into a circle and place on a greased baking tray

Mark (don't cut) into 4 equal pieces

Bake in a hot oven (200 degrees C) for 20 minutes

Fried Bannocks

Serves 4

<u>What you will need</u>:

1 cup plain flour

1 tablespoon of sugar

1 teaspoon of baking powder

A quarter of a teaspoon of salt

A quarter of a cup of cold milk

2 tablespoons of lard (or vegetable oil if preferred)

<u>What you will need to do</u>:

Mix all of the ingredients together to form a batter.
Oil your hands and split the mixture into 4 balls

Flatten the balls

Heat a deep frying pan and melt the lard

Fry the flattened balls until golden on each side

Fruit Bannocks on the Stane (for baking on a bannock stone next to a campfire… you can use a heavy baking tray)

Serves 4

<u>What you will need</u>:

1 cup plain flour

1 cup of mixed fruit (sultanas, currants, raisins)

1 tablespoon of sugar

1 teaspoon of baking powder

A quarter of a teaspoon of salt

A quarter of a cup of cold milk

<u>What you will need to do</u>:

Mix the flour, sugar, salt, fruit and baking powder together then stir in the milk. Mix thoroughly into a sticky dough. Pat onto the stone or into the tray and bake, turning once, until cooked through

Scones

Savoury and sweet versions

Potato scones (version 1)

Serves 4

<u>What you will need</u>:

450g of cold cooked mashed potato

Approximately half a cup of flour

A half a teaspoon of salt

<u>What you will need to do</u>:

Add the salt and the flour to the mashed potatoes and knead into a dough.

Cut into 4 and form into rounds.

Make 4 triangles from each round and brown both sides on a hot girdle or non-stick frying pan.

Special Potato scones (version 2)

Serves 4

<u>What you will need</u>:

Half a cup of oatmeal

450g of cooked, mashed potatoes

A half teaspoon of salt

2 tablespoons of flour

<u>What you will need to do</u>:

To the mashed potatoes, add the salt and the oatmeal and mix in the flour.

Roll out thinly and cut into triangles.

Cook on a hot girdle or non-stick frying pan, turning once and ensuring they are browned on both sides.

Sour Scones

Serves 4-6

<u>What you will need</u>:

<u>Pre-</u>soak a cup of oatmeal with a cup of buttermilk, cover and store in the fridge for a few days.

A cup of flour

A teaspoon of sugar

A teaspoon of caraway seeds

<u>What you will need to do</u>:

Mix the flour into the milk and oatmeal, add the sugar and the caraway seeds. Make into a soft dough, roll out and cut into rounds. Bake on the girdle or frying pan. Cook them steadily on the one side for about 5 minutes. You will see them begin to rise. Turn and give them about 5 minutes on the other side.

Cheese scones

Serves 6

What you will need:

200g of self-raising flour

Half a teaspoon of dry mustard

Half a teaspoon of salt

50g of butter

125g of grated cheese

1 egg

Tablespoon of water

What you will need to do:

Sift the flour, salt and mustard into a bowl. Rub in the butter and add the grated cheese. Use a little of the water and mix. Roll out onto a floured board (one inch thick). Cut into rounds and brush with beaten egg. Bake in a hot oven (200 degrees C) until you see that they have well risen (10 to 15 minutes)

Wholemeal scones

Serves 8-10

What you will need:

250g of wholemeal flour

250g of self-raising flour

A half teaspoon of salt

400mls milk

50g of butter

1 egg

What you will need to do:

Sift the flour and rub in the butter. Add the salt and mix through with the milk (ensure the mixture is not too wet)

Form into a dough and turn out onto a floured board

Roll to 1 inch thick and cut into 12 - 15 scones.

Brush with the beaten egg and bake at 200 degrees C for approximately 15 minutes

Herb scones

Serves 8-10

What you will need:

500g of self-raising flour

Half a teaspoon of salt

A shake of pepper

1 teaspoon of mixed herbs

50g of butter

1 egg

200mls of milk

What you will need to do:

Sift the flour, salt and pepper into a bowl. Rub in the butter and add the mixed herbs and the milk. Turn out onto a floured board and roll to one inch thick. Cut into rounds and brush with the beaten egg. Bake at 200 degrees C for approximately 15 minutes.

Sultana scones

Serves 8-10

<u>What you will need</u>:

500g of self-raising flour

Half a teaspoon of salt

1 tablespoon of caster sugar

1half a cup of sultanas

50g of butter

1 egg

200mls of milk

<u>What you will need to do</u>:

Sift the flour, salt and sugar into a bowl. Rub in the butter and add the sultanas and the milk. Turn out onto a floured board and roll to one inch thick. Cut into rounds and brush with the beaten egg. Bake at 200 degrees C for approximately 15 minutes.

Apple scones

Serves 8-10

Follow the recipe for sultana scones but replace the
sultanas with 1 grated apple

White girdle scones

Serves 8

<u>What you will need</u>:

450g of flour

A teaspoon of cream of tartar

A half a teaspoon of salt

A cup of buttermilk

<u>What you will need to do</u>:

Sieve the flour into a bowl and add the other ingredients to make a soft dough.

Turn out onto a floured board, roll and cut into 4.Flatten each piece into a round scone and divide these into quarters.

Flour and bake on a hot girdle or non-stick frying pan and turn when they are well risen and going brown on the one side. They should cook for about 5 minutes on both sides.

Treacle scones

Serves 6-8

<u>What you will need</u>:

1 cup of flour

2 tablespoons of butter

Half a teaspoon of baking soda

Half a teaspoon of cream of tartar

Half a teaspoon of cinnamon

Half a teaspoon of ground ginger

A pinch of salt

1 tablespoon of treacle

Half a cup of milk

<u>What you will need to do</u>:

Rub the butter into the flour and add the baking soda, the cream of tartar, cinnamon, ginger and salt. Mix thoroughly.

Melt the treacle in a little of the milk and stir into the mixture. Add just enough of the remaining milk to make a firm dough.

Turn out onto a floured board and knead lightly then roll out 3mm thick and cut into triangles.

Bake in a greased tin in a hot oven (200 degrees C) for 10 to 15 minutes.

Clap scones

Serves 6

<u>What you will need</u>:

1 cup of flour

A half teaspoon of salt

Boiling water

Honey

<u>What you will need to do</u>:

Sieve the flour into a bowl and add the salt. Pour over as much boiling water as necessary to make a pliable dough.

Roll into very thin rounds (as thin as you can make them) and pat with flour if required.

Bake on a hot girdle or non-stick frying pan.

It is important that, when nearly cool, you pile them one on top of the other and roll them. They should not be kept flat. Store temporarily in a tea towel.

Serve with honey.

Drop scones (also known as Scotch pancakes)

What you will need:

1 cup of plain flour

Half a teaspoon of baking soda

1 teaspoon of cream of tartar

1 tablespoon of caster sugar

2 eggs

Half a cup of milk

What you will need to do:

Sift the flour, sugar, baking soda and cream of tartar into a bowl. Beat the eggs and add them with the milk to the bowl. Mix to a batter

Spoon the mixture onto a hot, greased griddle (or thick frying pan)

The scones will rise and bubble. Turn when golden on the one side and gently brown on the other.

Sweet Puddings and Pies

Eve's Pudding

Serves 6-8

<u>What you will need</u>:

8 large cooking apples

400g of self-raising flour

400g of brown sugar

1 cup of raisins

300g of unsalted butter

6 eggs

<u>What you will need to do</u>:

Peel, core and slice the apples.

Grease a large serving dish with some of the butter

Place the sliced apples in the dish and scatter the raisins on top.

Beat the remaining butter and sugar together until it is creamed then beat in the eggs. Carefully fold in the flour then spread the batter over the apples

Bake for approximately 45 minutes

Queen of Puddings

Serves 6

<u>What you will need</u>:

Three quarters of a pint of milk

50g of butter

The rind of a lemon

1 tablespoon of caster sugar

1 cup of fresh white breadcrumbs

2 eggs

1 tablespoon of jam

<u>What you will need to do</u>:

Bring the milk nearly to the boil then add the butter, the lemon rind and the half of the sugar

Separate the eggs

Put the breadcrumbs in a bowl and pour over the hot mixture and stir in the egg yolks

Leave to stand for 10 minutes then pour it into a lightly greased pie dish (2 pint dish)

Bake in a moderate oven (180 degrees C) for approximately 20 minutes (until set)

Cover the pudding with the jam

Whisk the egg whites and pour over the pudding

Sprinkle the remaining sugar on top

Reduce the oven to 150 degrees C and return the pudding

Bake for a further 15 minutes (until the top is a toasted a light gold.

Almond Florry

Serves 6

What you will need:

450g of finely crushed almonds

900g of rough puff pastry

Quarter of a cup of orange flower water

8 eggs

Half a cup of cream

Half a glass of brandy

200g of clarified butter

450g of currants

2 tablespoons of sugar

A teaspoon of ground cinnamon

A half a teaspoon of nutmeg

What you will need to do:

Blanch the almonds in the orange flower water.

Separate the eggs and discard 4 of the egg whites. Beat the remaining 4 yolks with the other 4 eggs and mix in the cream, the brandy, the butter, currants, sugar, cinnamon and nutmeg.

Line a dish with half of the rough puff pastry and pour in the mixture. Cover with the remaining pastry and bake in a hot oven for 45 minutes or until the pastry is cooked.

Apple Florry

Serves 6

<u>What you will need</u>:

8 apples

900g of rough puff pastry

2 tablespoons of sugar

2 tablespoons of orange marmalade

A cup of water

A teaspoon of ground cinnamon

The rind of one lemon

<u>What you will need to do</u>:

Melt the sugar in the water. Add the cinnamon and

Peel, core and slice the apples and add to the sugar water. Simmer for 5 minutes then add the lemon rind.

Line a dinner plate with half of the pastry and cover with the apples. Spread over the marmalade and cover with the remaining pastry.

Bake in a hot oven for 45 minutes or until the pastry is cooked.

Prune Florry

Make as apple florry but replace the apples with 500g of stoned prunes and add a squeeze of lemon and a tablespoon of port.

Apple Pudding

Serves 4

<u>What you will need</u>:

6 apples

900g of rough puff pastry

170g of butter

4 eggs

A tablespoon of orange flower water

A tablespoon of brandy

1 teaspoon of sugar

The rind of one lemon

2 leftover plain biscuits

<u>What you will need to do</u>:

Peel, core and grate the apples and add the butter and beat until it resembles thick cream.

Beat the eggs and add to the mixture. Mix in the orange water, the brandy and the sugar.

Grind the biscuits and add to the mix with the sugar. Mix thoroughly.

Line a pie dish with pastry and add the mix. Cover with the remaining pastry and bake in a hot oven for 45 minutes or until the pastry is cooked.

Biscuit Pudding

Serves 4-6

<u>What you will need</u>:

6 leftover biscuits

2 cups of milk

4 eggs

1 cup of sugar

1 tablespoon of butter

1 teaspoon of vanilla extract

<u>What you will need to do</u>:

Break up the biscuits and soak in a cup of milk and stand for 10 minutes then beat in one of the eggs and the sugar. Beat in the remaining eggs one at a time.

Melt the butter and add to the mixture. Then add the remaining cup of milk and he vanilla extract.

Pour into a buttered pudding dish and put in a preheated moderate oven for 50 minutes or until a knife pushed into the middle comes out clean and dry.

Drumlanrig Pudding

Serves 4-6

What you will need:

6 stalks of rhubarb

Half a loaf of bread

Sugar to taste

What you will need to do:

Stew the rhubarb in sugared water. Layer the bread into a greased pudding basin and add the rhubarb. Add another layer of bread and then more rhubarb. Continue layering until the dish is full. Cover with a large plate and leave for 24 hours in the fridge.

(You can make this dish with raspberries, strawberries and currants instead of the rhubarb|.)

Apple Puddings in Skins

Serves 6

What you will need:

6 apples

4 leftover biscuits

1 cup of minced suet

1 tablespoon of sugar

1 glass of white wine

A teaspoon of ground cinnamon

Half a teaspoon of nutmeg

1 tablespoon of butter

What you will need to do:

Do not peel the apples but use a corer to remove each of the cores.

Pound the biscuits and add the suet, the sugar. The cinnamon and the nutmeg and mix in the wine. Spoon the mixture into the apples but not too full as it will swell.

Place side by side on a greased baking tray and share the tablespoon of butter by placing a small knop on the top of each apple.

Put in a moderate oven for 20 minutes or until the apples are cooked through.

Clootie Dumpling (version 1)

Serves 12

<u>What you will need</u>:

450g of flour

Half a cup of shredded suet

Half a cup of fresh breadcrumbs

Half a cup of sugar

1 teaspoon of mixed spice

Half a teaspoon of salt

A grated apple

1 cup of sultanas

One and a half cups of raisins

1 tablespoon of golden syrup

250mls of milk

<u>What you will need to do</u>:

Mix all of the ingredients thoroughly.

Scald a cloth in boiling water and dust with flour

Place the mixture on the cloth and tie securely but ensure that you leave plenty of room for the mixture to swell.

Place a plate on the bottom of a large pan of boiling water and place the pudding on top of the plate.

Cover and boil for 3 to 4 hours, topping up with boiling water throughout.

When cooked, remove the cloth gently and dry out the pudding for a few minutes in the oven.

Clootie Dumpling (version 2)

Serves 12

<u>What you will need</u>:

450g of flour

Half a cup of shredded suet

Half a cup of brown sugar

1 teaspoon of mixed spice

1 teaspoon of cinnamon

Half a teaspoon of salt

A grated apple

450g of mixed fruit (sultanas, raisins, currants)

Half a teaspoon of bicarbonate of soda

2 tablespoons of treacle

250mls of full fat milk

<u>What you will need to do</u>:

In an extra-large bowl, mix the flour, fruit, sugar, spice, cinnamon, suet and bicarbonate of soda

Add the salt, the treacle and some of the milk (enough to make the mixture slightly sloppy)

Scald a cloth in boiling water and dust finely with flour

Put the mixture on the cloth and secure with string (leaving enough room to allow the mixture to swell)

Place a plate in the bottom of a large pan of boiling water and place the pudding on top of the plate

Half fill the pan with boiling water.

Cover and boil for 3 to 4 hours, topping up the water throughout.

When cooked, remove gently from the cloth and dry out the pudding for a few minutes in a pre-heated oven.

Currant Duff

Serves 6

<u>What you will need</u>:

400g of flour

1 cup of shredded suet

1 cup of currants

Half a cup of caster sugar

Finely grated rind of 1 orange

Water

<u>What you will need to do</u>:

Sift the flour into a bowl and stir in the suet, currants, rind and sugar.

Stir in enough water to make a medium consistency batter. Butter a pudding basin and add the mixture and steam for two and a half hours then turn onto a warm plate.

Apple Meringue Pie

<u>What you will need</u>:

<u>For the flan case</u>:   250g of plain flour

125g butter

2 tablespoons caster sugar

1 egg yolk

1 tablespoon cold water

<u>For the apple meringue:</u>

6 apples

100g brown sugar

125g white sugar

2 tablespoons of jam (preferably plum)

2 tablespoons of flour

2 tablespoons of cream

1 egg yolk and 2 egg whites

<u>What you will need to do</u>:

<u>For the flan:</u> brush a flan tin with melted butter ((9 inch flan tin)

Sift the flour and rub in the butter until it resembles fine breadcrumbs then add the sugar. Add the egg yolk and the water and mix to form soft dough.

Wrap in cling-film and rest in the fridge for 20 minutes then roll out, line the flan tin and prick all over with a fork.

Blind bake (cover with greaseproof paper and weigh down with the weights of choice (baking beads, dried beans, dried rice etc.). Bake for 30 minutes at 180 degrees C.

For the apple meringue:

Peel, core and thinly slice the apples and place in the flan case.

Beat the egg yolk with the cream and then mix in the brown sugar and the flour. Pour and spread the mixture over the apples.

Bake in a hot oven (220 degrees C) for 10 minutes, reduce the heat to 180 degrees C and bake for a further 20 minutes

Make the meringue by whisking the egg whites and gradually adding the sugar. Spread the jam over the apple and top the pie with the meringue.

Bake in the oven (180 degrees C) for twenty minutes

Drunken Rhubarb and Whisky Pie

What you will need:

Make the flan case (see the flan recipe for apple meringue pie)

500g of rhubarb

75mls of whisky

1 tablespoon of caster sugar

1 egg yolk

Half a teaspoon of ground ginger

What you will need to do:

Bake the flan as per the recipe only use a 7 inch flan tin (and keep the spare pastry to one side)

Cut the rhubarb into small chunks and place in the flan case. Sprinkle over the whisky, the sugar and the ground ginger

Use the remaining pastry to place narrow strips across the rhubarb (twists of pastry look nice)

Put the pie back in the oven and bake for 20 minutes or until the rhubarb has softened

Cakes and Sweet Loaves

Fruit Cake (version 1)

Serves 6

<u>What you will need</u>:

340g of plain flour

170g brown sugar

170g sultanas

170g currants

170g raisins

50g chopped cherries

280ml milk

30g candied peel

Half a teaspoon mixed spice

Half teaspoon cinnamon

Quarter of a teaspoon nutmeg

70g butter

Teaspoon bicarbonate of soda

<u>What you will need to do</u>:

Sift the flour and mix in the spices

Rub in the butter and sugar and then add the fruit and the peel

Gently heat the milk to take the chill off and mix in the bicarbonate of soda then mix thoroughly through the cake mix

Grease a 17cm square baking tin,

Add the mixture

Bake at 180 degrees C for one hour, reduce the heat and bake for a further hour at 160 degrees C

Fruit Cake (version 2 – with whisky)

Serves 6

What you will need:

400mls of malt whisky

30g of ground almonds

200g of self-raising flour

170g brown sugar

600g of mixed fruit (sultanas, currants, raisins)

100g of mixed peel

3 eggs

A teaspoon mixed spice

Half teaspoon cinnamon

Quarter of a teaspoon nutmeg

150g butter

Teaspoon bicarbonate of soda

What you will need to do:

Soak the fruit in the whisky for at least 12 hours (longer if possible). If left in the fridge, remember to bring back to room temperature before adding to the mix

Cream the butter and sugar

Whisk the eggs and gently stir into the creamed mixture

Add the fruit and the whisky

Sift the flour and mix in the spices and the almonds then add to the mixture and mix thoroughly

Rub in the butter and sugar and then add the fruit and the peel

Grease and line a square baking tin, add the mixture and bake in a pre-heated oven (180 degrees C) for one hour and then cover the top with foil and bake for a further 45 minutes

Black Bun (this is an extremely rich fruit cake that will help to soak up the alcohol consumed on Hogmanay)

<u>What you will need</u>:

<u>For the pastry case:</u> (the cake is baked in a loaf tin that has been lined with the pastry)

340g of plain flour

170g of butter

Pinch of salt

Half a teaspoon of baking powder

Half a cup of Cold water

<u>For the cake</u>:

170g of plain flour

500g of raisins

500g of currants

Teaspoon of allspice

Teaspoon of ground ginger

Teaspoon of cinnamon

Teaspoon of baking powder

One tablespoon brandy

One large, beaten egg
2 tablespoons of milk

What you will need to do:

For the pastry:

Sift the flour and rub in the butter then add the salt.
Add enough of the water to form a firm dough (it has
to be firm to line the loaf tin and hold the cake)

Roll out the pastry

You need to place the pastry in the loaf tin in pieces,
so roughly measure the bottom, the 4 sides and the
top cut it into 6 appropriate lengths

Place the bottom and 4 sides in the tin – ensuring
the sides overlap. Keep the remaining (top) until you
add the cake mixture

For the cake:

Sift the flour and add the sugar, all of the fruit, the peel, the spices and the almonds and mix thoroughly then bind the mixture together by adding the brandy and half of the beaten egg. Add some milk to further moisten.

Once it is thoroughly mixed, put into the pastry case and add the pastry lid. Use the remaining egg to seal the edges and to create a glaze.

Prick the surface all over with a fork and use a skewer to place 4 holes from the lid to the base.

Bake for approximately three hours in a low to moderate oven (160 degrees C)

Montrose Cakes

What you will need:

100g of self-raising flower
100g of caster sugar
100g of butter
75g of currants
1 tablespoon brandy
quarter of a teaspoon of ground nutmeg
2 eggs

2 teaspoons of rose water

What you will need to do:

Beat the eggs. Cream the butter and sugar then add the eggs. Mix thoroughly then add the currants, the brandy, the rose water and nutmeg. Stir in the flour.

When thoroughly mixed, share and spoon the mixture into 24 paper cases (cupcake cases) which have been placed in cupcake tin and bake in a hot oven (190 degrees C) for 10 to 15 minutes

Marmalade Cake

<u>What you will need</u>:

226g of self-raising flour

2 eggs

2 tablespoons of milk

75g of caster sugar

100g of butter

2 tablespoons of marmalade (preferably orange)

1 teaspoon of finely grated orange rind

<u>What you will need to do</u>:

Sift the flour and rub in the butter until the mixture resembles fine breadcrumbs then add the sugar and the orange rind. Beat the eggs and add to the mix then add the marmalade and the milk

Mix thoroughly

Grease a 6 inch cake tin and add the mixture

Bake in a moderate oven (170 degrees C) for approximately 80 minutes

Dundee Cake

What you will need:

226g of plain flour

75g of butter

140g of caster sugar

Tablespoon of finely chopped almonds

12 blanched whole almonds (split in 2)

4 eggs

Teaspoon of baking powder

500g of mixed fruit (sultanas, raisins, currants)

Tablespoon of mixed peel

2 tablespoons of whisky

For the glaze – 2 tablespoons of warm milk sweetened with a teaspoon of sugar

What you will need to do:

Cream the butter and sugar and slowly add the eggs and most of the flour (a spoonful at a time) then add the chopped almonds and the fruit and the remaining flour Mix through the whisky and ensure everything is mixed thoroughly.

Put the mixture in a greased and lined 8 inch cake tin and cover with greaseproof paper. Bake in a moderate oven (170 degrees C) and after one hour, remove the paper and add the milk glaze then place the split almonds on top and bake for a further hour.

Gingerbread Loaf

<u>What you will need</u>:

22g of butter

200g of brown sugar

200g of treacle

500g of self-raising flour

2 teaspoons of powdered ginger

1 teaspoon of baking soda

200mls of milk

<u>What you will need to do</u>:

Cream the butter, sugar and treacle

Sieve the flour and the ginger and add to the treacle mix. Add the baking soda and some of the milk (enough to make a soft consistency)

Grease a 2lb loaf tin

Bake in a moderate oven (170 degrees C) for 90 minutes

Sultana Loaf (version 1)

Serves 6

<u>What you will need</u>:

500g of plain flour

1 teaspoon bicarbonate of soda

200g of butter

200g of brown sugar

200g of sultanas

3 eggs

300ml milk

<u>What you will need to do</u>:

Sift the flour and mix in the bicarbonate of soda then rub the butter into the flour until it resembles breadcrumbs

Add the sugar and the sultanas and then mix through the milk. Add the beaten eggs

Turn out into a greased 2lb loaf tin

Bake in a moderate oven (180 degrees C) for 90 minutes or until fully cooked through

Sultana Loaf (version 2)

Serves 6

<u>What you will need</u>:

250g of plain flour

250g of wholemeal flour

2 teaspoons of mixed spice

1 teaspoon bicarbonate of soda

170g of butter

200g of brown sugar

200g of sultanas

1 egg

300ml milk

<u>What you will need to do</u>:

Sift the plain and wholemeal flour with the spice and mix in the bicarbonate of soda then rub the butter into the flour until it resembles breadcrumbs

Add the sugar and the sultanas and then mix through the milk. Add the beaten egg

Turn out into a greased 2lb loaf tin

Bake in a moderate oven (180 degrees C) for 90 minutes or until fully cooked through

Bran Loaf

Serves 6

What you will need:

112g of All Bran cereal

280g of mixed fruit (sultanas, currants, raisons)

280ml of milk

140g of caster sugar

112g of self-raising flour

What you will need to do:

Mix the bran, fruit and sugar in a bowl

Add the milk and allow to stand and soak through for 30 minutes

Mix in the flour

Grease and line a 2lb loaf tin and add the mixture

Bake in a moderate to high oven (180 degrees C) for 60 minutes

Cool in the tin

Currant Duff

Serves 6

<u>What you will need</u>:

400g of flour

1 cup of shredded suet

1 cup of currants

Half a cup of caster sugar

Finely grated rind of 1 orange

Water

<u>What you will need to do</u>:

Sift the flour into a bowl and stir in the suet, currants, rind and sugar.

Stir in enough water to make a medium consistency batter. Butter a pudding basin and add the mixture and steam for two and a half hours then turn onto a warm plate.

Boiled Fruit Loaf (version 1)

Serves 6-8

What you will need:

230g of self-raising flour

112g of butter

112g of sugar

340g of mixed fruit (sultanas, currants and raisons)

1 egg

140mls water

What you will need to do:

Put the butter, fruit, sugar and water into a saucepan and mix thoroughly

Bring to a gentle boil and simmer for 20 minutes

Cool and then beat the egg and add to the mix

Mix in the flour and when thoroughly mixed, pour into a lined and greased 2lb loaf tin

Bake in a moderate oven (160 degrees) for 90 minutes

Boiled Fruit Loaf (version 2)

Serves 8-10

What you will need:

450g of self-raising flour

2 cups of sultanas

225g of butter

2 cups of milk

2 eggs

1 teaspoon of bicarbonate of soda

What you will need to do:

Mix the sultanas, milk, sugar and butter together in a saucepan and bring to a gentle boil

Simmer for 5 minutes

Cool and then mix in the flour and bicarbonate of soda. Beat the eggs and add to the mix

Share the mixture between 2 x 1lb loaf tins

Bake in a moderate oven (160 degrees) for 45 minutes to 60 minutes

Date and Walnut Loaf

Serves 10-12

<u>What you will need</u>:

12 oz. self-raising flour

8oz butter

80z dark brown sugar

8oz walnuts

340g dates (ensure thoroughly de-stoned)

1 teaspoon bicarbonate of soda

Half a pint of water

2 eggs

<u>What you will need to do</u>:

Put the butter, sugar and dates into a saucepan and add the water then bring to a gentle boil. Simmer for 5 minutes

Cool and mash and then add the bicarbonate of soda. Chop the walnuts and add to the mix

Beat the eggs and add to the mixture then add the the flour

Grease 3 x 1lb loaf tins and share the mix between the tins

Bake in moderate oven (160 degrees C) for 60-90 minutes

Raisin Tray-Bake

Serves 12

<u>What you will need</u>:

450g plain flour

225g butter

Water

450g raisins

1 teaspoon mixed spice

Half teaspoon cinnamon

Dessert spoon cornflour

1 tablespoon of sugar

Icing sugar

1 cup of desiccated coconut

<u>What you will need to do</u>:

Make the pastry by mixing the flour and butter to a fine breadcrumb consistency and add enough cold water to bind. Wrap in cling-film and chill for at least 30 minutes in the fridge

Put the raisins in a large saucepan and add sugar, mixed spice and cinnamon

Cover with water, bring to a gentle boil and simmer for 5 minutes

Mix cornflour with a little water and add to the mix to thicken

Allow to cool

Roll out pastry

Grease a large baking tray and line with the pastry

Add the cooled fruit

Bake in a moderate oven (180 degrees) for approximately 30 minutes.

Make up (thin) glace icing using the icing sugar and water

When the bake is completely cool cover with the icing and sprinkle on the desiccated coconut

Shortbread and Biscuits

Shortbread (version 1)

<u>You will need:</u>

240g of plain flour

120g of cornflour

120g of icing sugar.

225g of butter

Caster sugar for sprinkling on top

<u>What you will need to do:</u>

Cream the butter and the icing sugar until it is smooth and creamy. Sieve the flour and mix in until it forms a dough.

Rest the dough wrapped in cling film in the fridge for 20 minutes.

To roll – place between two sheets of cling film and roll out quite thick (half an inch at least).

Cut into fingers or rounds (for petticoat tails, put in a round baking tin and mark out lightly with a knife)

Prick the surface with a fork and bake in a moderate to high oven (190 degrees C) for about 20 minutes or until they are a pale golden colour.

Sprinkle with sugar and cool on a wire tray.

Shortbread (version 2 – chocolate chip)

<u>What you will need:</u>

200g of plain flour

25g of cocoa

200g of butter

100g of chocolate chips

85g of caster sugar

<u>What you will need to do</u>:

Make as version I, but sift the cocoa with the flour
and add the chocolate chips to the mix at the dough
stage.

Shortbread (version 3 – stem ginger)

What you will need:

200g of plain flour

100g of caster sugar

200g of butter

100g of semolina

2 teaspoons of ground ginger

8 pieces of stem ginger

Teaspoon of brown sugar

What you will need to do:

Make as version 1, but sift the semolina and the ground ginger with the flour then chop the stem ginger and add to the mix at the dough stage.

Shortbread (version 4 – caramel)

<u>What you will need:</u>

<u>For the shortbread base:</u>

200g of plain flour

150g of butter

75g of caster sugar

<u>For the filling</u>:

25g of butter

25g of brown sugar

A tin (397g) of condensed milk

<u>For the topping:</u>

<u>200g of milk chocolate</u>

<u>What you will need to do:</u>

<u>For the shortbread base:</u>

Sieve the flour and rub in the butter until the mixture resembles fine breadcrumbs. Mix in the sugar. Line a 9 inch square sandwich tin with greaseproof paper then pour in and firm down the mixture. Bake in a moderate oven (170 degrees C) for approximately 30 minutes or until golden brown.

Allow to cool

<u>For the filling</u>:

Add the condensed milk, the butter and the sugar to a pan and gently heat – stirring continuously – until the mixture thickens then spread the mixture over the (cooled) shortbread base and allow to cool

<u>For the topping:</u>

Melt the chocolate and spread over the (cooled) filling and allow to set

Cut into squares

Empire Biscuits

For empire biscuits use the recipe for shortbread (version 1) but roll out thinner and cut into rounds. Bake for less time and remove just as the biscuits are changing colour (keep a close eye on them and remove from the oven as SOON as they change colour. These biscuits burn very quickly. They may appear soft, but the will crisp up as they cool)

When cool (cool on a wire tray) sandwich with raspberry jam and cover with icing (glace – icing sugar and water).

Oaties (version 1)

<u>What you will need:</u>

112g of plain flour

2 teaspoons of baking powder

Half teaspoon of salt

112g of rolled oats

50g of caster sugar

75g of treacle

112g of butter

<u>What you will need to do</u>:

Sieve the flour, baking powder and salt and add the rolled oats. Heat the sugar, treacle and butter in a pan until melted then mix it into the flour. Mix thoroughly and then press into a 7 inch greased sandwich tin and bake in a moderate oven (170 degrees C) for 20 minutes.

Cut into wedges and cool on a wire tray.

Oaties (version 2)

30mls of melted bacon fat

A quarter of a teaspoon of bicarbonate of soda

A quarter of a teaspoon of salt

200g of rolled oats

Two tablespoons of warm water

What you will need to do:

Mix the majority of the oats, the bicarbonate of soda and the salt together with the melted bacon fat and mix to a dough with the water.

Put the remaining oats on a board and turn out the dough onto the board, knead and then roll out into a thin round

Cut into 3 triangles (farls) and cook on an ungreased girdle (or heavy frying pan) until crisp (not brown) turn and cook for a minute on the other side.

Tantallon Biscuits

What you will need:

112g of plain flour

112g of rice flour

A pinch of baking soda

112g of butter

112g of sugar

2 eggs

3 drops of lemon essence

What you will need to do:

Beat the eggs. Sieve the plain flour, the rice flour and the baking soda. Cream the butter and the sugar and then mix a little of the egg with a spoonful of the flour mix and continue until all ingredients are thoroughly combined then add the lemon essence and stir in.

Roll out thinly and cut into rounds

Bake on a greased baking sheet in a moderate to hot oven (180 degrees C) for 30 minutes

Cool on a wire tray

Abernethy Biscuits

What you will need:

225g of plain flour

Half a teaspoon of baking powder

100g of butter

100g of caster sugar

1 teaspoon of caraway seeds

1 egg

A tablespoon of milk

What you will need to do:

Sieve the flour and the baking powder and rub in the butter and then add the sugar and the caraway seeds. Beat the egg and add to the mix and add the milk to form a stiff dough. Roll out thinly on a floured board and cut into rounds.

Bake on a greased baking sheet in a moderate oven (160 degrees C) for 10 minutes

Ginger Biscuits

<u>What you will need:</u>

112g of self-raising flour

2 teaspoons of ground ginger

10g of caster sugar

Half a teaspoon of bicarbonate of soda

112g of butter

112g of golden syrup

A tablespoon of milk

<u>What you will need to do:</u>

Sieve the flour, sugar, bicarbonate of soda and the ginger.

Add the syrup and the butter to a pan and melt without boiling. Cool and add the mix.

Roll mixture into small balls and place on a greased baking sheet. Allow plenty of space between as the balls will spread.

Dip a pastry brush in the milk and use it to slightly flatten the balls.

Bake in a low to moderate oven (160 degrees C) for 10 minutes. They should be firm but not hard.

Cool on a wire tray

Walnut Biscuits:

What you will need:

200g of plain flour

150g of caster sugar

1 teaspoon of baking powder

112g of butter

50g of finely chopped walnuts

1 egg

What you will need to do:

Beat the egg. Sieve the flour and the baking powder and rub in the butter until it resembles fine breadcrumbs. Add the caster sugar and the walnuts and add the egg.

Turn out onto a floured board and knead thoroughly before rolling out thinly and cutting into rounds

Bake on a greased baking sheet in a moderate to hot oven (190 degrees C) until golden brown (should only take 5 or 10 minutes)

Cool on a wire tray

If you enjoyed these recipes, take a look at

My Wee Granny's Old Scottish Recipes by Angela Hossack

Plain, delicious and wholesome Scottish fare from my Wee Granny's table to yours

Contents:

Base Stocks

Soups

Fish Dishes

Catsups, Stuffing and Sauces

Poultry

Game and Other Meat Dishes

Bridies and Pies

Vegetable Dishes

Puddings and Tarts

Bannocks and Scones

A word about Shortbread

Made in the USA
Columbia, SC
07 December 2018